Our
Friend
Mikayla

Written and Illustrated by Mikayla's Third-Grade Classmates

at Lower Nazareth Elementary School
in Nazareth, Pennsylvania

"Mikayla taught us that people with disabilities aren't really different and that they can do just about everything. They just do things in a special way. And they can be a very good friend, like Mikayla is to us. Now that we know Mikayla and understand about what having a disability really means, we want to tell Mikayla's story. So we wrote this book so everyone could know about Mikayla. And so everyone could understand about her disabilities. All kids should know not to be afraid of someone like Mikayla. It does not matter if someone is in a wheelchair. Their disability doesn't mean you cannot be friends. Having a friend with a disability is cool. Just like being friends with Mikayla is cool. We hope everyone can hear her story and that everyone can have a friend just like her."

–*Mikayla's third-grade class, Lower Nazareth Elementary School*

"I am tremendously proud of Mikayla's friends at Lower Nazareth Elementary School. I am still amazed by their total acceptance of Mikayla and the special bond they have with her. When she was assigned to a traditional class we hoped that inclusion would be a positive experience for our daughter and her classmates, but it has far exceeded our expectations. Mikayla's friends have made a real difference in her life, and with this book hopefully they will encourage other children to do the same for someone with a disability."

–*Kimberly Resh, Mikayla's mom*

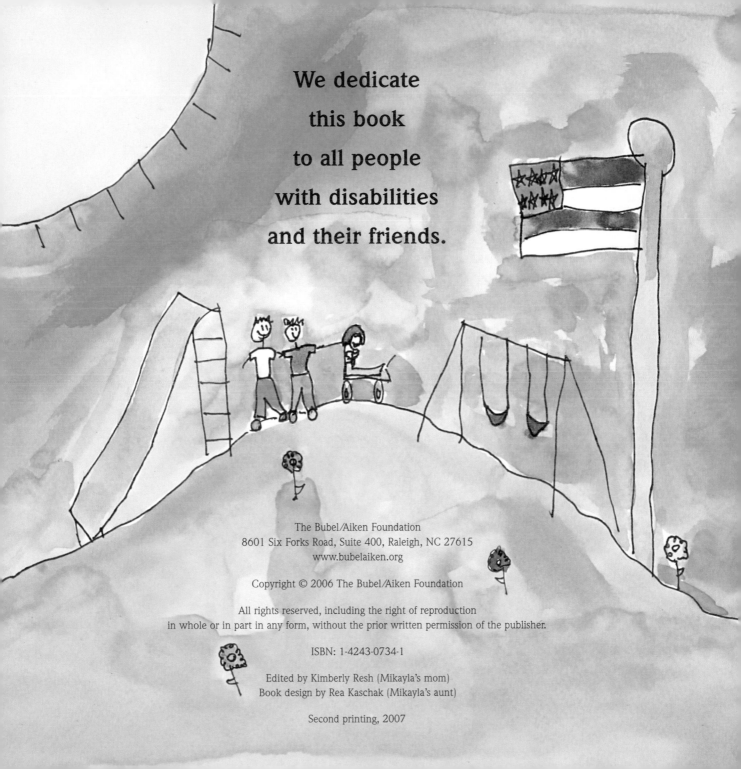

We dedicate
this book
to all people
with disabilities
and their friends.

The Bubel/Aiken Foundation
8601 Six Forks Road, Suite 400, Raleigh, NC 27615
www.bubelaiken.org

ISBN: 1-4243-0734-1

Edited by Kimberly Resh (Mikayla's mom)
Book design by Rea Kaschak (Mikayla's aunt)

Second printing, 2007

Mikayla is a girl in our third-grade class.

She is in a wheelchair

and has a lot of disabilities.

But that does not mean

we cannot be friends.

ABCDeFghIJKlmnopqrstuvwxyz

Mikayla needs a ramp to help her

get in and out of her mom's mini-van.

When our class goes on a field trip,

she uses a school bus with a special lift

that works like an elevator.

Mikayla rides in her wheelchair

up the ramp or lift

to get in the mini-van or bus.

She stays in her wheelchair for the ride,

but she still uses a seat belt!

Mikayla can't eat with her mouth

so she has a tube that goes right into her belly.

Her mom feeds her special milk through her tube.

She can still taste things like lollipops,

and her favorite treat is cotton candy.

Mikayla can't hear very well,

but she can hear us.

We love talking to her.

She can't see very well,

but she can see bright colors.

She can see red and yellow the best.

We use bright-colored markers and crayons

to color pictures for her.

Mikayla has "brain damage."

Before she was born,

when Mikayla was still in her mom's belly,

she didn't get enough air.

Because she didn't get enough oxygen to her brain,

her brain was injured.

Her brain doesn't send the right messages

to her legs, her arms,

and the other parts of her body she can't use.

That is why she can't walk or talk

and has trouble seeing and hearing.

When we first saw Mikayla,

we were surprised because we had never had

a kid in our school in a wheelchair.

Most of us stared at her

because we didn't know what had happened.

We wanted to know what was wrong with Mikayla.

We had never met a kid with a disability.

We felt shy.

Most of us were also a little afraid

when we first met her.

We felt scared because

we thought Mikayla was different

and not like a "normal" kid.

We were afraid of what she had.

One of us even thought it was contagious,

but we learned it's not.

There is nothing to be scared of.

We felt bad for Mikayla

because she has brain damage

and is in a wheelchair.

We didn't know how to talk to her.

We thought she would not be able to

play games or sports with us.

We had no clue how to be Mikayla's friend.

But now we know.

It's much easier than we thought.

On Mikayla's first day of third grade,

her mom came in and told us about her.

She answered all our questions.

When we thought of new questions,

we asked our teachers.

We also asked other kids

who had known Mikayla before.

After a few weeks, we got used to Mikayla.

We weren't scared anymore because

we learned there is nothing to be afraid of.

We felt happy because we had never had

a friend with disabilities.

Now we do.

Mikayla is our friend.

We help push her to class.

We sit with Mikayla at lunch and talk to her.

At recess we push her in her special swing.

Kids with disabilities like to do

the same things we do.

Mikayla likes to listen to music.

She watches "American Idol" with her family.

She is a Clay Aiken fan.

Last summer she even saw Clay in concert!

Mikayla goes to the mall

and shops at the same stores we do.

She wears the same kinds of clothes,

and she might even get her ears pierced.

We think she should!

Mikayla can even do some sports.

She roller-skates at "Skateaway."

She uses her wheelchair to skate

because she has wheels on the bottom of it.

Someone just has to push her around.

Mikayla is a cheerleader.

She likes to cheer.

Every game she wears her uniform

and brings her pom-poms.

The other girls hold her hands

and help her shake them.

She has signs on her wheelchair that say

"Go Wildcats!" and stuff like that.

Mikayla goes bowling.

Instead of throwing the ball,

she drops the ball down a special ramp.

Someone helps her push the ball off.

The ball will roll all the way down

to hit the bowling pins.

In gym class,

she can use the bowling ramp

to pitch when we play kickball.

It was our idea to have Mikayla be the pitcher.

Mikayla talks to us by hitting her "switch."

Her switch is a button you put on her wheelchair.

Whenever she turns her head to hit it,

the switch controls whatever it is hooked up to.

She uses her switch to talk

by playing a recorded message.

Mikayla has to practice hitting her switch

so it gets easier for her.

Mikayla can work almost anything with her switch.

She has a special spinner with all our names on it.

By using her switch, Mikayla spins the spinner

to pick which of us will be her helper for the day.

She uses her switch to play games,

like the math bingo game.

By hitting her switch to make a fan work,

Mikayla can blow out the candles on her birthday cake.

She also uses her switch to cook.

Her sister holds the mixer

while Mikayla powers it with her switch.

From Mikayla, we've learned that

people with disabilities aren't really different.

Mikayla is no different from anyone else.

She does things in a special way,

but she can do just about everything we can.

Now that we know more about Mikayla,

we feel silly that we were afraid of her.

She is just like us.

We are glad Mikayla can do things we can

and are happy we made a new friend.

We hope Mikayla is in our class again.

If we meet someone who doesn't know Mikayla,

we will introduce her.

We will tell them what happened to Mikayla

and explain about her disabilities.

Even if we have to explain over and over again, we will...

because they might be afraid

just like we were when we met her.

We will tell other kids not to be scared,

that Mikayla is nice,

and it's fun to have her as a friend.

It doesn't matter if your friend

is in a wheelchair.

Their disabilities don't mean

you cannot be friends.

Having a friend with a disability is cool.

Sometimes the world needs a voice. Let it be yours.

The Bubel/Aiken Foundation envisions a world where young people with developmental disabilities are totally immersed in all life has to offer. We encourage a society where both typical children and those with developmental disabilities can enjoy the activities of life together. Inclusion makes us all stronger. Our mission is to open the world to children who have often been left on the sidelines of life. By inviting them in, we gain the opportunity to expand our concept of what 'ability' means and broaden what we offer one another in a society that will be made more whole because of its diversity.

"I want to send a personal thank you to the children of Lower Nazareth Elementary School. The story that they tell through *Our Friend Mikayla* is inspiring and demonstrates what true inclusion brings to those who experience it. By sharing their story, they've raised their voices for children everywhere and given us the view of what an inclusive world can offer all of us."

–Clay Aiken

"As a mother of a child with a developmental disability, I've experienced what it is like for a child to feel a sense of exclusion. *Our Friend Mikayla* tells the story of a child fully included in the world of typical children. It's a wonderful story and a message I hope extends beyond their school and into the hearts of children and adults everywhere."

–Diane Bubel

–background painted by Mikayla

Bubel Aiken *foundation*

To learn more about
The Bubel/Aiken Foundation
or ways to get involved visit
www.bubelaiken.org